DISNEY SONGS FOR RAGTIME PIANO

5 CLASSIC TUNES ARRANGED BY PHILLIP KEVEREN

ISBN 978-1-4950-9973-1

— PIANO LEVEL —
LATE INTERMEDIATE

Disney Characters and Artwork © Disney

Walt Disney Music Company
Wonderland Music Company, Inc.

DISTRIBUTED BY

7777 W. BLUEMOUND RD. P.O. BOX 13819 MILWAUKEE, WI 53213

In Australia Contact:
Hal Leonard Australia Pty. Ltd.
4 Lenatara Court
Cheltenham, 3192 Victoria, Australia
Email: ausadmin@halleonard.com.au

Visit Hal Leonard Online at
www.halleonard.com

Visit Phillip at
www.phillipkeveren.com

PREFACE

I have wonderful memories of visiting Disneyland® Resort as a kid. The "big" attractions (they were called "E" Tickets back then!) like Space Mountain and the Matterhorn Bobsleds were certainly highlights, but I particularly loved Main Street, U.S.A. – and the best part of Main Street, U.S.A. was the ragtime piano player. I spent many hours over the years listening to the superb musicianship of these pianists, wondering if I could ever possibly get my left hand to stride with such ease. It seemed like there was no tune request they could not fill. It was pure fun and high-flying virtuosity wrapped in a sparkling package!

When I was asked to write a book of Disney tunes in ragtime style, it was the easiest "yes" ever. Are you kidding?! I started that very day – and you are holding the result of that phone call. Before playing any of these arrangements, give a listen to some vintage ragtime (Joplin's "Maple Leaf Rag," et al.) to get in the proper headspace. It's a fun place to be!

Sincerely,

Phillip Keveren

BIOGRAPHY

Phillip Keveren, a multi-talented keyboard artist and composer, has composed original works in a variety of genres from piano solo to symphonic orchestra. Mr. Keveren gives frequent concerts and workshops for teachers and their students in the United States, Canada, Europe, and Asia. Mr. Keveren holds a B.M. in composition from California State University Northridge and a M.M. in composition from the University of Southern California.

CONTENTS

4	**THE BARE NECESSITIES**	THE JUNGLE BOOK
10	**BE OUR GUEST**	BEAUTY AND THE BEAST
7	**CRUELLA DE VIL**	101 DALMATIANS
14	**I JUST CAN'T WAIT TO BE KING**	THE LION KING
18	**IT'S A SMALL WORLD**	IT'S A SMALL WORLD® ATTRACTION AT DISNEYLAND® RESORT AND MAGIC KINGDOM® PARK
22	**LITTLE APRIL SHOWER**	BAMBI
24	**MICKEY MOUSE MARCH**	THE MICKEY MOUSE CLUB
26	**ONE JUMP AHEAD**	ALADDIN
33	**SUPERCALIFRAGILISTICEXPIALIDOCIOUS**	MARY POPPINS
36	**TOPSY TURVY**	THE HUNCHBACK OF NOTRE DAME
40	**UNDER THE SEA**	THE LITTLE MERMAID
44	**YO HO (A PIRATE'S LIFE FOR ME)**	PIRATES OF THE CARIBBEAN® ATTRACTION AT DISNEYLAND® RESORT AND MAGIC KINGDOM® PARK
30	**YOU CAN FLY! YOU CAN FLY! YOU CAN FLY!**	PETER PAN
51	**YOU'LL BE IN MY HEART** (POP VERSION)	TARZAN™*
48	**ZIP-A-DEE-DOO-DAH**	SONG OF THE SOUTH

THE BARE NECESSITIES

from THE JUNGLE BOOK

Words and Music by
TERRY GILKYSON
Arranged by Phillip Keveren

CRUELLA DE VIL
from 101 DALMATIONS

Words and Music by
MEL LEVEN
Arranged by Phillip Keveren

Sneaky (♩ = 120)

BE OUR GUEST

from BEAUTY AND THE BEAST

Music by ALAN MENKEN
Lyrics by HOWARD ASHMAN
Arranged by Phillip Keveren

I JUST CAN'T WAIT TO BE KING

from THE LION KING

Music by ELTON JOHN
Lyrics by TIM RICE
Arranged by Phillip Keveren

With a strut (♪ = 138)

IT'S A SMALL WORLD

from Disneyland® Resort and Magic Kingdom® Park

Words and Music by RICHARD M. SHERMAN
and ROBERT B. SHERMAN
Arranged by Phillip Keveren

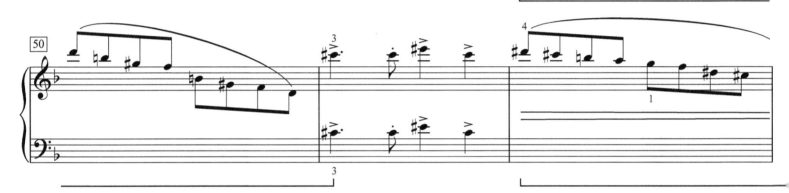

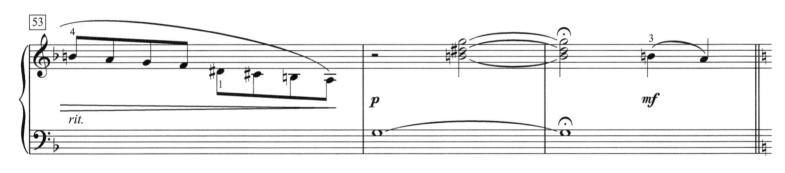

LITTLE APRIL SHOWER
from BAMBI

Words by LARRY MOREY
Music by FRANK CHURCHILL
Arranged by Phillip Keveren

MICKEY MOUSE MARCH

from THE MICKEY MOUSE CLUB

Words and Music by
JIMMY DODD
Arranged by Phillip Keveren

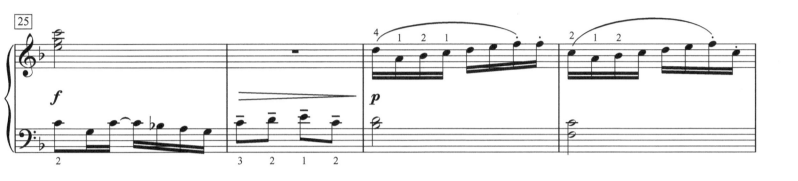

ONE JUMP AHEAD

from ALADDIN

Music by ALAN MENKEN
Lyrics by TIM RICE
Arranged by Phillip Keveren

YOU CAN FLY! YOU CAN FLY! YOU CAN FLY!

from PETER PAN

Words by SAMMY CAHN
Music by SAMMY FAIN
Arranged by Phillip Keveren

SUPERCALIFRAGILISTICEXPIALIDOCIOUS
from MARY POPPINS

Words and Music by RICHARD M. SHERMAN
and ROBERT B. SHERMAN
Arranged by Phillip Keveren

TOPSY TURVY

from THE HUNCHBACK OF NOTRE DAME

Music by ALAN MENKEN
Lyrics by STEPHEN SCHWARTZ
Arranged by Phillip Keveren

UNDER THE SEA

from THE LITTLE MERMAID

Music by ALAN MENKEN
Lyrics by HOWARD ASHMAN
Arranged by Phillip Keveren

YO HO
(A Pirate's Life for Me)
from PIRATES OF THE CARIBBEAN® at Disneyland® Resort and Magic Kingdom® Park

Words by XAVIER ATENCIO
Music by GEORGE BRUNS
Arranged by Phillip Keveren

ZIP-A-DEE-DOO-DAH
from SONG OF THE SOUTH

Words by RAY GILBERT
Music by ALLIE WRUBEL
Arranged by Phillip Keveren

YOU'LL BE IN MY HEART
(Pop Version)
from TARZAN™

Words and Music by
PHIL COLLINS
Arranged by Phillip Keveren

THE PHILLIP KEVEREN SERIES

PIANO SOLO

00156644 **ABBA for Classical Piano** $15.99
00311024 **Above All** $12.99
00311348 **Americana** $12.99
00198473 **Bach Meets Jazz** $14.99
00313594 **Bacharach and David** $15.99
00306412 **The Beatles** $19.99
00312189 **The Beatles for Classical Piano** $17.99
00275876 **The Beatles – Recital Suites** $19.99
00312546 **Best Piano Solos** $15.99
00156601 **Blessings** $14.99
00198656 **Blues Classics** $14.99
00284359 **Broadway Songs with a Classical Flair** $14.99
00310669 **Broadway's Best** $16.99
00312106 **Canzone Italiana** $12.99
00280848 **Carpenters** $17.99
00310629 **A Celtic Christmas** $14.99
00310549 **The Celtic Collection** $14.99
00280571 **Celtic Songs with a Classical Flair** $12.99
00263362 **Charlie Brown Favorites** $14.99
00312190 **Christmas at the Movies** $15.99
00294754 **Christmas Carols with a Classical Flair** $12.99
00311414 **Christmas Medleys** $14.99
00236669 **Christmas Praise Hymns** $12.99
00233788 **Christmas Songs for Classical Piano** $14.99
00311769 **Christmas Worship Medleys** $14.99
00310607 **Cinema Classics** $15.99
00301857 **Circles** $10.99
00311101 **Classic Wedding Songs** $12.99
00311292 **Classical Folk** $10.95
00311083 **Classical Jazz** $14.99
00137779 **Coldplay for Classical Piano** $16.99
00311103 **Contemporary Wedding Songs** $12.99
00348788 **Country Songs with a Classical Flair** $14.99
00249097 **Disney Recital Suites** $17.99
00311754 **Disney Songs for Classical Piano** $17.99
00241379 **Disney Songs for Ragtime Piano** $17.99
00364812 **The Essential Hymn Anthology** $34.99
00311881 **Favorite Wedding Songs** $14.99
00315974 **Fiddlin' at the Piano** $12.99
00311811 **The Film Score Collection** ... $15.99
00269408 **Folksongs with a Classical Flair** $12.99
00144353 **The Gershwin Collection** $14.99
00233789 **Golden Scores** $14.99
00144351 **Gospel Greats** $14.99
00183566 **The Great American Songbook** $14.99
00312084 **The Great Melodies** $14.99
00311157 **Great Standards** $14.99
00171621 **A Grown-Up Christmas List** ... $14.99
00311071 **The Hymn Collection** $14.99
00311349 **Hymn Medleys** $14.99
00280705 **Hymns in a Celtic Style** $14.99

00269407 **Hymns with a Classical Flair** $14.99
00311249 **Hymns with a Touch of Jazz** $14.99
00310905 **I Could Sing of Your Love Forever** $16.99
00310762 **Jingle Jazz** $15.99
00175310 **Billy Joel for Classical Piano** $16.99
00126449 **Elton John for Classical Piano** $19.99
00310839 **Let Freedom Ring!** $12.99
00238988 **Andrew Lloyd Webber Piano Songbook** $14.99
00313227 **Andrew Lloyd Webber Solos** $17.99
00313523 **Mancini Magic** $16.99
00312113 **More Disney Songs for Classical Piano** $16.99
00311295 **Motown Hits** $14.99
00300640 **Piano Calm** $12.99
00339131 **Piano Calm: Christmas** $14.99
00346009 **Piano Calm: Prayer** $14.99
00306870 **Piazzolla Tangos** $17.99
00386709 **Praise and Worship for Classical Piano** $14.99
00156645 **Queen for Classical Piano** $17.99
00310755 **Richard Rodgers Classics** $17.99
00289545 **Scottish Songs** $12.99
00119403 **The Sound of Music** $16.99
00311978 **The Spirituals Collection** $12.99
00366023 **So Far...** $14.99
00210445 **Star Wars** $16.99
00224738 **Symphonic Hymns for Piano** $14.99
00366022 **Three-Minute Encores** $16.99
00279673 **Tin Pan Alley** $12.99
00312112 **Treasured Hymns for Classical Piano** $15.99
00144926 **The Twelve Keys of Christmas** $14.99
00278486 **The Who for Classical Piano** $16.99
00294036 **Worship with a Touch of Jazz** $14.99
00311911 **Yuletide Jazz** $19.99

EASY PIANO

00210401 **Adele for Easy Classical Piano** $17.99
00310610 **African-American Spirituals** $12.99
00218244 **The Beatles for Easy Classical Piano** $14.99
00218387 **Catchy Songs for Piano** $12.99
00310973 **Celtic Dreams** $12.99
00233686 **Christmas Carols for Easy Classical Piano** $14.99
00311126 **Christmas Pops** $16.99
00368199 **Christmas Reflections** $14.99
00311548 **Classic Pop/Rock Hits** $14.99
00310769 **A Classical Christmas** $14.99
00310975 **Classical Movie Themes** $12.99
00144352 **Disney Songs for Easy Classical Piano** $14.99
00311093 **Early Rock 'n' Roll** $14.99
00311997 **Easy Worship Medleys** $14.99
00289547 **Duke Ellington** $14.99
00160297 **Folksongs for Easy Classical Piano** $12.99

00110374 **George Gershwin Classics** $14.99
00310805 **Gospel Treasures** $14.99
00306821 **Vince Guaraldi Collection** $19.99
00160294 **Hymns for Easy Classical Piano** $14.99
00310798 **Immortal Hymns** $12.99
00311294 **Jazz Standards** $12.99
00355474 **Living Hope** $14.99
00310744 **Love Songs** $14.99
00233740 **The Most Beautiful Songs for Easy Classical Piano** $12.99
00220036 **Pop Ballads** $14.99
00311406 **Pop Gems of the 1950s** $12.95
00233739 **Pop Standards for Easy Classical Piano** $12.99
00102887 **A Ragtime Christmas** $12.99
00311293 **Ragtime Classics** $14.99
00312028 **Santa Swings** $14.99
00233688 **Songs from Childhood for Easy Classical Piano** $12.99
00103258 **Songs of Inspiration** $14.99
00310840 **Sweet Land of Liberty** $12.99
00126450 **10,000 Reasons** $16.99
00310712 **Timeless Praise** $14.99
00311086 **TV Themes** $14.99
00310717 **21 Great Classics** $14.99
00160076 **Waltzes & Polkas for Easy Classical Piano** $12.99
00145342 **Weekly Worship** $17.99

BIG-NOTE PIANO

00310838 **Children's Favorite Movie Songs** $14.99
00346000 **Christmas Movie Magic** $12.99
00277368 **Classical Favorites** $12.99
00277370 **Disney Favorites** $14.99
00310888 **Joy to the World** $12.99
00310908 **The Nutcracker** $12.99
00277371 **Star Wars** $16.99

BEGINNING PIANO SOLOS

00311202 **Awesome God** $14.99
00310837 **Christian Children's Favorites** $14.99
00311117 **Christmas Traditions** $10.99
00311250 **Easy Hymns** $12.99
00102710 **Everlasting God** $10.99
00311403 **Jazzy Tunes** $10.95
00310822 **Kids' Favorites** $12.99
00367778 **A Magical Christmas** $14.99
00338175 **Silly Songs for Kids** $9.99

PIANO DUET

00126452 **The Christmas Variations** $14.99
00362562 **Classic Piano Duets** $14.99
00311350 **Classical Theme Duets** $12.99
00295099 **Gospel Duets** $12.99
00311544 **Hymn Duets** $14.99
00311203 **Praise & Worship Duets** $14.99
00294755 **Sacred Christmas Duets** $14.99
00119405 **Star Wars** $16.99
00253545 **Worship Songs for Two** $12.99

Prices, contents, and availability subject to change without notice.

HAL•LEONARD®

Search songlists, more products and place your order from your favorite music retailer at **halleonard.com**

Disney characters and artwork TM & © 2021 Disney LLC

0422
158